CW01648293

Crystals & Healing for Everyone

2nd Edition

❖

Henriette Maasdijk
FMFSEM, MAST, Cert Ed

Vibrational Healing Foundation

Published by:
The Vibrational Healing Foundation
London W1A 6US

Second Edition

First Edition published in the UK in 2004

A catalogue record of this book
is available from the British Library.

ISBN 978 0 9547569 1 8

Disclaimer
The information in this book is based upon the author's personal knowledge and experience and is not intended to diagnose, prescribe or treat any ailment, nor is it intended as a substitute for qualified medical advice. If you have a medical problem, or emotional, mental or spiritual health concerns, please consult a qualified physician or a medical healthcare professional. This information is presented at this time with no claim of scientific proof.

All information and techniques are to be used at the sole discretion of the reader. Throughout the book, all exercises have been recommended in good faith. Therefore, in the event that you use the information in this book, the author and publisher assume no responsibility for your actions. This book is for personal use only. Those who wish to use crystals for healing others should obtain a recognised qualification.

Cover Design by Mark Williams
Photography © Vibrational Healing Foundation

For information about courses:
vibrationalhealingfoundation.co.uk

To all who have guided me, and to those who have come for guidance.

Contents

Foreword

The beauty of the Mineral Kingdom has attracted humankind since ancient times. Their use as items of jewellery and as aspects of art and architecture are well documented. What is less known is that there is historical reference that points to their use as potent healing tools in almost every culture.

The renewed interest in crystals today has brought an explosion in the vast array available, and it can be quite overwhelming when entering a crystal shop to know where to start, especially as a beginner. Many people are perplexed as to which crystal to buy and what to do with it once they have it!

Hundreds of books have been written on the subject offering advice and techniques to adopt, but what is sometimes overlooked, is the need to understand that crystals are extremely powerful tools and should be used with caution. This is one of the aspects that is addressed in this book.

Henriette Maasdijk is the Founder of The Vibrational Healing Foundation and The Federation of Subtle Energy Medicine. She has a profound intrinsic understanding and respect for the Mineral Kingdom and how to use this knowledge in regard to subtle energy medicine. In her book she draws on her experience of over thirty years of working with crystals to offer clear, precise exercises and techniques that can be utilised safely by both a beginner and more experienced therapists alike.

This book is the beginning of a journey of exploration that can take the reader into the fascinating world of crystals and the wisdom they offer us, if we will just but listen.

Julia Marafie

Introduction

Many years ago, I was asked by quite a number of people, including those who sold crystals at health and wellness shows, to write a simple and easy to read book about how to use crystals in daily life, since at the time, there were few books on this topic. Having already created a booklet on the subject, I elaborated on this with the inclusion of a number of self-healing exercises for the newcomer. This made its way into print, in 2004, as 'Crystals and Healing for Everyone'.

The feedback I received was extremely positive not just from newcomers but also from students and graduates in the field of crystal healing who, to date, find it serves them well as a reference book. In addition to this, the book can be used as a summary for those who might choose to attend a workshop or short course on the subject of crystals and healing. Although the book has been out of print for a while, I was made aware that there is still a demand for it and so decided to bring out a second edition.

I have taken the opportunity to update the information, add to the healing techniques and lists of crystals, and correct an embarrassing amount of spelling mistakes. The book has also been restructured to be more readable, and photographs of each crystal have been added, in a visual guide, for identification purposes.

Crystals and minerals are not just amazingly beautiful, but they also form the cornerstone of our physical world, and without them we would not exist. In addition to this, they are invaluable tools for subtle energy healing and inner development, provided they are used with respect and expertise. I hope this book inspires you to explore the world of crystals and thereby have fun as well as enrich your daily life. I wish you much joy on your crystal & self-healing journey!

Henriette

PART I

UNDERSTANDING YOUR CRYSTALS

1

The Mineral Kingdom

The beauty of crystals and gemstones has inspired humanity since ancient times. Precious stones have always been regarded as status symbols as well as an expression of wealth and power. The crown jewels of various countries and church regalia encrusted with beautiful gemstones are only some examples of this.

Crystals and minerals have also been used in the past to create brilliant colours in paints, which we can still admire in old master paintings, icons and frescoes. Some were also finely ground and ingested as medicine or used as eye makeup. Crystals have been known for their healing properties since the beginning of time and were used as such in many different cultures and civilisations.

In order to gain an understanding of the ancient art of crystal healing, it is important to become aware of the fact that the Mineral Kingdom is the first and foremost on this planet. Together with the elements of air, water and fire, it is the cornerstone upon which all other life is built. One could also argue that the earth itself is partially crystalline, since the crust is almost entirely made up of minerals. Most of these originate from deep within the earth whilst others were formed at or near the surface. This process, which has been going on for millions of years, is still continuing, and like everything else, is also forever changing and evolving.

Not only are we surrounded by crystals and minerals, but they also form part of our bodies and encompass our daily living. You can find them everywhere in nature: in caves; mountains; seas and riverbeds; on beaches; near volcanoes; and deep within the earth. The North and South Poles are covered in snow and ice, which is nothing else but crystallised water. We have many crystalline substances, as well as trace elements, within our bodies: for instance, Apatite is in our bones and teeth.

We also eat crystals! Rock Salt or Halite is one of the most common crystals on the planet. And nowadays, crystals are widely used in industry and modern technology. Most of us wear jewellery made of precious or semi-precious stones or metals such as gold, silver or copper. We may also have pretty ornaments made of crystalline substances in our homes, or buy them as gifts for our friends and relatives. Crystals and minerals have always been part of us and our daily life, and they always will be.

What distinguishes minerals from anything else in nature, is their inner regular atomic structure. When this manifests on the outside in beautiful geometrical shapes, they are called crystals, otherwise, the term is crystalline or massive. Crystals can actually be regarded as the most orderly structure in the whole of nature. Some stones have no inner orderly structure and are known as amorphous (without form). An example of this is Obsidian, a natural glass. Other natural glasses are Tecktites, such as Moldavite, which is a pale to dark green glass created by the impact of a meteor in Romania many years ago.

Amber and Jet are materials that are sometimes mistaken for crystals. Amber is fossilised tree resin and Jet is composed from rotted and compressed trees. Another substance originating from trees is Fossilised or Petrified Wood. This is segments of ancient trees that have crystallised.

Opal is another stone that is technically not a crystal. It consists of small spheres of Silica surrounded by water. This is the reason why one should take care not to leave Opals in the hot sun or near a radiator. They might crack! Substances from the sea such as Coral, Abalone or Pearls are also at times mistaken for crystals, especially since they are often used for healing. They have a lighter energy than most other crystals and mainly impact through their colour. For practical purposes, all minerals and stones mentioned in this book will be termed crystals.

Although rarely used in healing work, ordinary stones have their own specific energy. This energy may be considered fairly basic, but stones do form part of the mineral kingdom and are therefore included in this book. Many of us inadvertently surround ourselves with stones: some people place bowls of stones on their coffee tables for decoration; granite worktops in kitchens are currently highly fashionable; and stones such as basalt are often used in combination with massage. As stated before, the energy of stones is fairly basic; however, it can have a healing effect albeit mild, and the author, herself, keeps a large pebble in her car, which helps her stay firmly grounded when driving.

In the last thirty years or so, there has been a revival of interest in the subject of crystal and other forms of energy healing, and many books, courses and workshops are currently available. Before embarking on a study of this, it is essential to first establish that crystal healing is complementary to conventional medicine and not an alternative. This form of healing is holistic, which means that the focus is on the individual as a whole, rather than on physical symptoms. Therefore, a simple explanation of both the human energy field and healing is necessary.

2

The Subtle Energy Field and Healing

All living things have an electromagnetic field around them known as the aura. For many hundreds of years, mystics, sensitives and healers (in the Western world), who were able to perceive this auric field, were ridiculed, persecuted or executed. It is only recently that science has proven that it must exist around every living organism, naming it the bio-magnetic field or bioenergy field. It is worthwhile to mention that it has been an established fact for over a hundred years, that everything and everyone in this world can be viewed as energy. In spite of this, there are still many sceptics who consider it a lot of rubbish. The reason for this may be that most human beings, although able to perceive energy, are usually unaware of it. An unpleasant atmosphere in a house, office or emanating from a person, is nothing else but negative energy. It is sensed by most but not recognised for what it is. The same goes for positive energy.

Throughout this book, the terms, human energy field, energy field, aura and auric field will be used interchangeably to describe the bioenergy field.

In Human beings, the aura consists of several layers and contained within it are a number of energy systems. The best known are the meridians, the chakras and the grid system. More about these later.

Our emotional, mental and spiritual makeup is held within our aura, and when we are healthy and well, the energies flowing through it are clear and balanced. Any form of disharmony, that we experience, can cause blockages or other disturbances in our energy field, and when these are not addressed, they may eventually manifest as physical symptoms or illness. In more simple terms, one could say that the condition of our physical body is but the expression of our emotional, mental and spiritual states of being.

Healing is about addressing such disturbances in someone's energy field. This can often trigger certain changes, insights or reactions on the recipient's part, which may then lead to the restoration of health and harmony. One could liken the various parts of the subtle energy field to an orchestra playing a beautiful piece of music. If one player is out of tune, it will upset the whole. By playing the correct note (made up of healing energies, crystals and other tools), the aforementioned player will follow suit. As in all healing, it is the built-in self-healing capability of a client that is activated, promoted or accelerated.

Being able to assess the condition of the various energy systems in someone's auric field takes a certain amount of training. To then apply appropriate crystals, to help bring anything untoward back into harmony, requires in-depth knowledge and practical experience in this specialist field. Since the energy systems relate to our life experiences, including our thoughts, feelings and memories, it follows that they are in constant motion. Equally, each individual is unique, and therefore one cannot generalise or set specific treatments with specific crystals. To illustrate this in more detail, a simple explanation of the energy field is necessary.

Meridians are a highly complex system of energy pathways running through the physical body and closely connected to various organs. Situated along these pathways, are numerous points which one could liken to mini-roundabouts. It is these points that are addressed by acupuncturists in order to free up congested energy. Working with crystals on this system is highly complex since it requires an in-depth knowledge of the meridian system, which is intricate in itself. Healers who work with this system usually hold a qualification in Acupuncture as well.

Chakras are vortexes of energy situated along the spinal column within the auric field. They can be described as cones or spirals of spinning energy, and they function on many levels. They also loosely relate to various glands, organs and body parts. They are interconnected, which means that the condition of one usually affects some of the others. At times, chakras can be spinning too fast, or they can be sluggish, damaged, traumatised, too open, full of debris and blocked, depending on what is going on in someone's life. Obviously, different crystals would have to be used in order to help balance any of these aforementioned states.

There also exists an energy grid which runs through the entire auric field and connects us to everything and everyone else. Certain parts of this grid relate to our personal state of being and can be out of balance according to what is occurring in our life. Although this system may seem less difficult to understand, assessing its condition and then using appropriate crystals to help bring it into balance, takes expertise and experience on the part of a healer.

All the systems are contained within the various layers of the auric field. Although most healers are aware of seven distinctive ones, for the purpose of this book, it will be sufficient to only mention four. The etheric body is the first layer. It is closest to the physical body and feeds it with energy and vitality. The emotional body is the second layer, and it is the seat of the emotions. To those who perceive energy, this layer contains many colours. The next two layers form the mental body. This is where all thought processes are apparent, including the subconscious mind. The outermost layers can be grouped into the spiritual body – the seat of higher ideals, our blueprint and our spiritual makeup.

Of the systems mentioned, the meridians have the most immediate effect upon the physical body. These are mainly situated within the physical and etheric bodies. The chakras spin through all the subtle bodies and can be addressed on various different levels according to what is going on in a person's life; and the grid system could be described as the most intangible since it is the most difficult to perceive. Should you be interested in learning more about 'subtle anatomy', it may be worthwhile to attend a suitable course or read up about it.

This book is written for newcomers and serves as a user-friendly introduction, which is why only safe, straightforward and easy to implement healing techniques are presented. Crystal healing techniques pertaining to the meridians, specific subtle bodies, chakras and the grid system require considerable skill and could be unsafe if tried out by the layperson. All the exercises in this book relate to various layers in the auric field and can help to achieve more harmony and balance. Please note that they are meant for personal use only. Those who wish to work more in-depth with crystals, or use them for healing others, will need professional training in order to be able to do so in an appropriate, effective and responsible manner.

Treat your crystals as you should treat yourself – with both love and respect.

3

The Uniqueness of Crystals

Because of their orderly structure, crystals can absorb, reflect, transform, transmute, balance, direct, amplify, soften, clear, shape and focus energies. Additionally, each crystal carries its own unique vibration that is the result of its chemical composition, colour frequency, inner atomic structure and outer form. Crystals come in a multitude of beautiful colours which is, of course, healing and uplifting in itself.

The chemical composition of crystals can interact with us on subtle levels since our physical form contains many of these minerals and trace elements. Often people intuitively choose crystals that contain a mineral they lack and then wear it for a while. The energy frequency of the mineral in question could well help to alleviate the deficiency as it occurs within the aura. Similarly, specific flower remedies can help with emotional difficulties. Please note that healers do not deliberately choose crystals for their mineral content since they do not focus on physical conditions. Another reason is that crystals are not a substitute for the intake of necessary minerals.

The colour frequency of crystals forms a significant component of their overall composition. Colour is an essential part of our lives and affects us on many levels. We take these vibrations in through our skin, eyes and auric field and also ingest them with our food. A few keywords relating to specific colours are:

Red
Grounding, vitality, stamina, purpose, warming, action, stimulating, passion, motivation, extrovert, self-confidence

Orange
Self-respect, joy, uplifting, vitality, releasing, creativity, tonic, replenishes, cheerful, spontaneous

Yellow
Joy, happiness, uplifting, will, concentration, enthusiasm, self-worth, energy, wisdom (Gold)

Green
Nature, balance, harmony, abundance, relaxation, sharing, stress, release, empathy, self-love, stabilising, going with the flow

Pink
Unconditional love, compassion, sensitivity, gentleness, nurturing, giving and receiving, kindness, openness, softness

Blue

Peace, loyalty, hope, honesty, soothes and calms, cooling, truth, release of tensions and aches, relaxing, communication, healing, self-expression

Indigo

Pain healer, profound understanding, wisdom, protection, vision, idealism, responsibility, sedative, cooling, seeker

Violet

Knowing, power, dignity, transforming, insight, freedom, cleanser of negativity, inspiration, spiritual growth, service

Black

Absorbs light, stability, security, drains excess energy, mastery, power, pain relief, grounding

White

Reflects light, clarity, purity, perfection, contains all colours, cleansing, innocence, clearing negativity

Turquoise

Refreshing, strengthening, communication, sparkling, encourages, replenishes, alertness, awareness, clarity of expression, stimulates

Crystal healing is different from colour therapy, since although an important factor, the colour of crystals is not the only one taken into consideration during a healing session. The causes of colour in crystals vary, which is why two crystals of different types, that display the same colour, usually carry different vibrations. To give an example, Citrine and Yellow Jasper, which are both yellow crystals, are so different in energy that they cannot be used for comparable conditions on the same areas within the subtle energy field. One is uplifting, and the other is grounding. Many crystals do, however, relate to the basic qualities of colour as described above. Rose Quartz has a nurturing quality, Aventurine is about balance and Blue Lace Agate can help ease tensions.

The regular inner atomic structure of crystals is another aspect of their overall makeup. When crystals form, their molecules arrange themselves into orderly patterns, depending on their inner atomic structure. All crystals can be categorised by their pattern, or *inner shape*, into what are known as crystal systems. There are seven of these: the **cubic** system is the most regular of these shapes; **tetragonal** is shaped like a shoebox; **monoclinic** is akin to a parallelogram; **orthorhombic** is a diamond shape; **triclinic** is the most irregular; **trigonal** is like a triangle; and **hexagonal** is hexagon shaped. Stones that do not have this regular structure are called **amorphous**.

This inner sacred geometry of crystals can help to instigate the healing processes on much deeper levels, and many healers use this esoteric knowledge in practice. For the layperson, it is also of interest, since it can explain why vastly dissimilar crystals often harmonise well. Amazonite and Rhodonite are but one example:

they share the same inner structure, but one is of the feldspar family, and the other is altogether different.

The outer form of a crystal is another part of its unique vibration. Natural crystals are very different from those that are polished or artificially shaped. They seem to be softer and more absorbing, whereas the energies of polished crystals are far more intense since a larger amount of light shines through. If one compares a gemstone such as Emerald, Ruby or Sapphire with the rough version, this is very apparent.

Crystals are often fashioned into specific forms such as cubes, wands, spheres, eggs, or pyramids. Each of these shapes is archetypal. The **cube**, for instance, represents the material world and can therefore help with being more grounded. **Wands** are directional and about focus, concentration, ritual and sometimes power. **Spheres** can represent wholeness, unity and infinity; **ovals** can be about fertility or protection (our aura is in the shape of an oval), and **pyramids** can help generate more energy or relate to change and protection. Therefore, in meditation, the shape may affect you as much as the energy of the crystal; it is important to be aware of this fact.

Apart from its incredible beauty, there is a magical life force as well as an innate intelligence expressed throughout the whole of the Mineral Kingdom. We can all tap into these qualities, provided we work with love, respect and integrity. Crystals can be enjoyed in daily life, and used for self-development and self-healing by anyone.

4

Choosing Crystals

Many crystals are purported to be helpful for a variety of conditions or have so-called traditional meanings, and although lists of their energetic qualities can be helpful as an initial guideline, they greatly oversimplify issues. This is because each of us is a unique being with different needs and requirements. One only needs to reflect upon the constant flow of emotions, thoughts, beliefs, habits, memories, ambitions and so on, that form part of each person's energetic makeup, to illustrate this fact. A crystal that can help one individual on subtle levels may therefore be unsuitable or ineffective for another.

It is important to mention that the notion that specific crystals can be used to treat or cure a variety of physical symptoms and diseases is misleading. Crystal healing is an energy therapy and not a physical therapy and must not be confused with conventional medicine, treatments or medication.

In view of the above, the most appropriate way to choose crystals for yourself is to use your intuition. The way to do this is by briefly focusing on the purpose for which you need or would like to use a crystal. So, if, for instance, you would like a crystal to help you sleep, focus for a moment on the question, "which crystal could help me sleep at night?" and then look at a collection of crystals.

The right one will stand out in a manner that is fairly obvious. It may be the colour that attracts you, the way light flows through it, or the shape or texture may appeal to you. It could have that extra sparkle and will definitely feel pleasant when you pick it up. You may, when holding a crystal for a little while, become aware of a resonance within your own being, or you may have an instant inner knowing that a specific crystal is the one you need.

It can happen that a crystal attracts your attention in no uncertain manner, even if you do not have a definite purpose for it in mind. In this case, it may be worthwhile to spend some time with it in order to find out why it chose you. The outcome could surprise you.

When there are numerous crystals displayed in a show or shop, it is often the very first one you notice that will leave with you an hour or two later. If you are choosing a crystal for your own well-being or healing, just focus on what is needed for your highest good and never on any symptoms or negative conditions.

To choose a crystal for a friend, focus on this person for a short while, picturing him or her well and happy. Mentally ask which crystal would be suitable for his or her highest good and then select the one that stands out the most. Above all, rather than relying on crystal lists or what other people may tell you, use your own intuition and trust it!

Clean Crystals
are
Happy Crystals!

5

Cleansing Crystals

It is very important to ensure that your crystals are clean, both physically and energetically, before you wear or use them. Crystals can absorb as well as transmit energies, and you do not want to risk introducing any form of negativity into your own energy field or your surroundings. Therefore, whenever you buy or are given a crystal, it is a good idea to spend some time with it and to clean it thoroughly. After all, you do not know where it has been, who has used or worn it, or how the mining process has affected it.

Following this initial cleansing, it is also necessary to clean the crystal before and after every use. Crystals you wear should be cleaned every day. Whenever your crystals look dull, listless or feel sticky, they are in need of cleansing. Equally, whenever you think, feel or wonder if one of your crystals is in need of a good clean, it is usually best to do so! Please do not forget to also clean your jewellery, including gold, copper and silver. Concerning jewellery that a family member or a friend may have left you in their will, please take extra care to thoroughly cleanse it, especially if any form of illness has been involved. You can then tune it for your highest good and enjoy wearing it.

There are countless methods for cleaning crystals. The most important aspect of this process is to focus on the intent (of cleansing) whilst you are doing so. This will ensure that the crystal is energetically as well as physically clean. You could, for instance, hold your crystal under running water for a few moments while concentrating on it being cleansed, or leave it for a few hours in a bowl of water. In this case, bless the water and ask that it may serve to clean your crystal.

Please note that crystals with a high metallic content can be adversely affected by water and lose their sheen. Some examples are Malachite, Turquoise, Pyrite and Hematite. Halite, a salt crystal, will dissolve in water, and powdery or fragile crystals are best cleaned using other methods.

Alternatively, you can place your crystals in a bowl of potpourri, pass them through incense, or put them on a larger crystal which is tuned for the purpose of cleansing. Sound can instantly shatter negative energies, so chiming a bell or Tibetan bowl over a crystal, or chanting into it with intent (of cleansing) is also a very good method.

You can visualise light flowing through your crystal, clearing it of any negativity, or gently blow on it provided, of course, you do not have a cold! Leaving your crystal in sunlight will both cleanse and energise it. Beware, the colour of some crystals does fade when placed in sunlight for a long period of time. Amethyst, Celestite and Fluorite are some examples. Equally, please be careful about leaving Clear Quartz in direct sunlight since it could act as a magnifier and set the place alight!

For heavy-duty cleansing, you can place your crystal in rock or sea salt, or bury it in a pot of earth for a while (not for fragile crystals). Please bear in mind that when you bury a crystal in your garden, it may well decide to go for a walkabout, never to be found again! It is a good idea to try out various methods and then use the ones you find most effective.

Crystals make good friends.
They listen to your laments and never complain.

6

Tuning Crystals

Having cleansed your crystal, you may wish to tune it for the purpose you chose it for. This is done by using thought or visualisation. Thought vibrations will interact with the energy frequencies within a crystal and fine-tune it according to need. For example, should you have acquired a crystal to help you sleep, just hold it for a while, concentrate on the matter at hand, and then mentally ask the crystal to help you with this.

When we concentrate on something specific, the mind forms pictures. This is why it is imperative to always focus on a positive outcome rather than a negative condition. When tuning your crystal to help you sleep, picture yourself as peacefully asleep rather than tossing and turning, and also think of the quality of sleep and not insomnia. You could then place the crystal on your night table, or if it is small, under your pillow. Sleep well!

Healers link to 'Universal Energies' and then tune their crystals for the highest good of their client prior to use. Afterwards, these crystals are cleared as well as cleansed (both with intent), and if not used for anything else, dedicated for good in general. This is done because nature abhors a void and will always seek to fill it, and we do not want our crystals to absorb random energies!

When tuning your crystals for a specific purpose, always affirm that it may be for the highest good of all concerned, or in the case of self-healing, for your own highest good. The reason for this is that whatever we do usually affects the lives of others, and we do not always know the bigger (or best) picture.

It is best to tune a crystal for just one specific purpose; this avoids confusion. If you want to change the purpose, cleanse the crystal and also focus on it being cleared. You can then re-tune it for something else.

7

Uses of Crystals in Daily Life

There are many ways in which crystals can help you in daily life – placing them around the house in order to create a harmonious atmosphere, is only one of them. They also interact well with plants, flowers and animals. Should, for instance, one of your plants be in a sorry state, you could tune a crystal to help heal it and then place it in or near the pot. Obviously, you must also continue to care for it yourself.

If you receive a bunch of fresh flowers, you may find it helpful to place a few crystals, tuned to help maintain the freshness of the flowers, around the vase, or place one in the water. If you have a garden, you could place a few crystals in strategic spots to help everything grow. Just be prepared to weed a lot! When your pets are unhappy or upset, you could place a suitable crystal in their basket or attach it to their collar. Of course, any ill pet must be taken to the vet for treatment, but you could then tune a crystal to help it recover.

Crystals can also help protect your energy field from negative influences so that you are less affected by the harmful emanations from computers, televisions or other appliances. When placing crystals on your computer or near any other electrical device, please make sure that they are properly tuned to either absorb, clear or neutralise the negative energies. If you do not do this, they could amplify the problem. You will also need to clean these crystals frequently since they can become very toxic indeed. Black Tourmaline is an excellent crystal for this purpose although Sodalite and most Quartz crystals (except Amethyst because it is fairly fragile) are also effective. Please note that the crystals will not eliminate the problem completely, they just help minimize the exposure.

Crystals can be used to help you concentrate or take in and give out knowledge, which is valuable for study or exams. Just tune one accordingly and have it with you whilst attending classes and when you are being assessed! Crystals can be of help in cultivating inner states of mind and emotions such as self-esteem, patience, confidence, joy or a positive attitude. When in need of any of these qualities, just tune an appropriate crystal and wear it or carry it with you. You could use crystals to help you remember your dreams or to wake you up in the morning in place of a noisy alarm clock. Please try this method out a few times before relying on it. For those who meditate, crystals can help to find that point of inner stillness and peace.

Nowadays, it is not always permitted to have fresh flowers or plants in hospital rooms. As an alternative, you could give a crystal to the patient in question, and tune it for his/her highest good and well-being. Both its beauty and energy could help accelerate the healing process, and this would not burden the nurses with additional work. Another use for a crystal could be to place it next to your phone and tune it to encourage callers to leave a clear message on the answering machine rather than hang up.

If you are a healthcare professional, or have an office where people come to discuss their problems, it is useful to have a few crystals around. Since crystals are also objects of beauty, there would be no need to explain their function to clients. Rose Quartz, tuned for harmony and nurturing, can help ease an atmosphere of apprehension, fear, anger or similar feelings; Amethyst can assist in absorbing negativity; while Apophyllite can aid in clearing it; and Jasper can help maintain stability and groundedness. Obviously, you would need to tune these crystals for their specific purpose and take a few moments to clear them every evening.

You could place crystals in your kitchen to help you cook more creatively. If you, like the author, are a little indulgent at times and use a small amount of Rock or Sea

Salt in your cooking, do not forget to tune it for the highest good of those who will eat it. Why not speak your troubles into a crystal instead of overburdening your friends? It is an excellent method for ridding yourself of tensions. Please do not forget to clean it afterwards and to give it a break, from time to time. It may also be a good idea not to let anyone hear you do this!

If you choose a crystal for your car, perhaps to help you find parking spaces or to focus better on your driving, please make sure it is a crystal with a grounding energy. You do not want to be spaced out when driving.

Necklaces, bracelets, earrings and rings are usually made up of crystals or crystalline substances. If you ensure that your jewellery is clean and properly tuned, it can be of great help to your overall well-being. Of course, this is also a good excuse to obtain a variety of jewellery so that every morning you can make a choice according to how you feel; just like choosing your clothes for the day.

Many ornamental objects, such as small containers, carvings of animals or other figurines, are made of crystals. Although already stunning to look at, they can also be tuned to help enhance the atmosphere in your home.

Crystals definitely make wonderful and welcome gifts. When you give a friend or a loved one a crystal, it is a good idea to show them how to clean and care for it, or to provide a few written instructions. The more you get involved with the fascinating world of crystals, the more you will be able to benefit from their inspiring energies.

8

Caring for Crystals

Crystals are so beautiful, it would be a shame to hide them away in cupboards or in a chest of drawers. Should you have collected an array of tumblestones and wish to place them in a bowl, it is important to be aware of their hardness in order to avoid damage. A (non-scientific) scale, created by (and named after) the Austrian mineralogist, Friedrich Mohs, is used for this. The scale rates hardness from one to ten, whereby one denotes the softest crystals and ten the hardest. A crystal or mineral with a low rating can be scratched by another which is higher on the scale.

It is interesting to note that dust has a hardness of seven. So, a piece of Fluorite (4) that is covered in dust (7) should not be wiped since the dust could scratch it. Blowing on it or holding it under running water would be a better cleansing method. A list of the hardness of the crystals covered in this book can be found in the appendix.

When deciding where to place crystals in your home, just use your intuition. If it 'looks right' it is right. If you are a collector of crystals, you may not wish to place too many large ones in your bedroom, especially if you are sensitive to their energies. It could interfere with your sleeping patterns, particularly if the large crystals are highly energising. Crystals that have a metallic content should not be placed in the bathroom nor Clear Quartz on the windowsill (see cleansing crystals). When you place crystals in your garden or patio, please note that weather conditions and pollution may affect the look of the crystal over a period of time.

PART II

SELF HEALING WITH YOUR CRYSTALS

9

Simple Self-Healing with Crystals

As mentioned before, crystals can also serve as a tool to help us with our overall health and well-being. You can select and tune crystals to help you relax, ease your tensions or aches, sleep, meditate, gain certain insights, ground, strengthen, and clear or energise yourself. There is no need to attend any lengthy classes or training to be able to do this. The exercises are simple and easy to use.

Grounding

Please note, that whenever you meditate, practice self-healing or work with crystals in an energetic sense, you may find yourself in a slightly altered state of awareness. For some people, this can be quite profound. It is, therefore, of the utmost importance to ground and focus your energies afterwards. It is best to do this with visualisation as well as physically. I would recommend that you also use grounding crystals during relaxation, meditation or any other self-healing exercises, in order to benefit on all levels.

To ground yourself with visualisation, imagine roots growing from the soles of your feet and the base of your spine, deep into the earth beneath you, which then spread out just like the roots of a large tree. You could then either place specifically tuned crystals beneath your feet or hold one or two in your hands. Suitable crystals could be the black, brown, red, orange, dark yellow and green ones, or those with a metallic sheen. There is a list of these in Chapter 14. To ground yourself in a more physical sense, focus for a moment on the in-breath, stretch your body and stand up. If you still feel a bit spaced out, you can clap your hands, stamp your feet or drink some water. Just make sure that you are fully alert and awake before continuing with your daily life.

Should you often feel spacey, have problems concentrating or be a bit of a daydreamer, it might be a good idea to wear an earthing crystal for a while. Some other indications of not being very grounded can be forgetfulness, an oversensitivity to noise or light, being unable to get your point of view across, or having many good ideas and never realising them. You can also become more focused and grounded without the use of crystals. Physical activities such as sports, exercise, walking or gardening always help. Wearing earthly colours like browns, greens, reds etc. are also a good idea.

Should you be extremely ungrounded, start by using crystals that are gentle grounders, rather than choosing the heavy-duty ones. To come down to earth with a bang can be highly unpleasant! To select the correct grounding crystal, just focus for a moment on the question, 'what could help me ground at this point in time?' and then choose. Be aware that over time this may change.

Relaxation

Nowadays, stress is unfortunately very much part of our daily lives, and it is important to fully relax both body and mind from time to time. Usually, crystals with a soft and gentle energy are appropriate for this. Make sure you will not be disturbed and either sit or lie down. Take a few deep breaths and then, holding your cleansed and tuned crystal and breathing normally, imagine that with each in-breath you take in the quality of peace or harmony, and on each out-breath you let go of any tension or disturbance. Continue to do this until each part of your being is in a state of complete relaxation. Should there be a persistent tension somewhere, it may help to briefly hold your crystal over that area and gently breathe light into and around the tenseness. Sometimes, focusing on a soft colour when doing this helps.

WARNING: If you have a pacemaker, do not place crystals upon or near your chest. Certain crystals, such as those from the Quartz family, are piezoelectric and may interfere with your pacemaker. Also, if you are pregnant, it is advised that you do not place crystals on your stomach. If you are unsure about whether to place a crystal on your body, please do not do so without consulting a qualified crystal & energy healer.

You could also hold your crystal whilst listening to peaceful music or a relaxation CD. If you are frequently stressed, you may find it helpful to do this at a specific time every day. Should this be difficult, just listen to it before going to sleep. It is not necessary to use crystals every time. Please note that if you cannot relax and become panicky whilst listening to the relaxation CD, you may need to see a stress therapist or stress healer in order to help you. Stresses and tension tend to build up over time and when not eased, will eventually affect the immune system and ultimately manifest as illness. It is, therefore, advisable to relax both mind and body at least once a day.

Meditation

There are many ways in which to meditate. All, however, have one thing in common: the need to empty your mind of random thoughts and the ability to be still. If you find this difficult, you could choose and tune a crystal to help you reach, and be in, that point of inner stillness. It may be worthwhile to point out that grounding and balancing crystals are often more appropriate for this than those with a very high and fast energy. Should you need any insight concerning a situation, hold a suitable crystal, sit in a comfortable place, close your eyes, calm your mind and then enter a meditative or reflective state by being still. A thought, symbol or flash of inspiration may shed some light on the issue, or you may feel a profound inner calm enabling you to take some distance.

Please note that whenever you meditate or work energetically with crystals, your auric field will expand. The ordinary state of the field in most people, who are going about their daily lives, is approximately 50 to 100 centimetres (around 1.5 to 3 feet) from the physical body to the outer edge. By grounding yourself after your energy work, your auric field should revert back to its natural state.

Linking

You can link to anything and anyone via thought. This includes qualities such as peace, harmony and joy, to name just a few. You can also link to Universal energies, your Higher Self, what some call your Guardian Angel, and so on, according to your own personal belief system. The way to do this is to first ground yourself, then imagine your egg of light around you, and follow this with affirming that you only wish to engage with, or link to, positive energies. You then enter into your inner, still space and focus on your intent. You could choose a crystal to help you with this, in line with your objective. As with all such exercises, do ground yourself afterwards and make sure you are back in an ordinary state of awareness.

Channelling

After linking, you can ask for healing energies (for your highest good and well-being) to flow through and around you. Some folk prefer to call these Light or Love energies. Just use a term that concurs with your faith or values. Many also ask the Angelic for help when doing this. Once the energies flow, you can let the surplus go into the earth beneath you. The flow of energy will stop automatically once you have received enough. Make sure you ground yourself at the end. It may be useful to point out that before you link to Light energies and channel these, it is important to first enter a profound state of peace and relaxation.

A Self-Healing Meditation

Select a crystal and ensure it is clean and tuned for your highest good, and for the healing that you need at this point in time. You may also need a couple of grounding crystals to place at your feet. Hold the crystal in your hand and become aware of a point of light above your head (or link to the Light and the Angelic, and ask to receive healing energies). Just know or imagine that rays of these 'Light and healing' energies are flowing through and around you, saturating you, your auric field and your crystal. Now imagine that the crystal you are holding is expanding and growing around you so that you are completely immersed in its energy. Stay in this state of healing and relaxation for a while, and when you feel it has been enough, thank the Light and become aware that the crystal you are holding has returned to its ordinary state. Ground yourself thoroughly and clean the crystals.

Protection

Many sensitive people, or those who work in the caring professions, often feel drained after having seen certain clients. Equally, some therapists may, at times, feel the symptoms of their clients within themselves. It can also happen that you feel threatened, upset or invaded by other people for no apparent reason. On the other hand, you could find that you are easily influenced by others, unable to say no when needed, or unnaturally fearful and defensive at times. All of the above are indications that your energy field is not as strong as it could be.

One way to change this is to tune a crystal to help protect and strengthen your aura. Hold the crystal and picture yourself within an oval shape of light (this is the natural shape of your auric field); then affirm that only positive and beneficial energies may enter your space. The lower part of the shape should be situated underneath you (within the ground) since this will also help you to be more grounded. If you like, you could also visualise the colour of your crystal surrounding you. Then hold the crystal for a while, carry it with you or wear it. Crystals with a high frequency colour such as purple, blue, turquoise, white, silver or gold can be helpful for this.

We all affect each other and are affected by our environment, and it is of vital importance to have a strong energy field in order to be able to stay balanced and healthy, and not take onboard anything untoward. It is necessary to point out that by doing this work you are not creating a barrier between yourself and others; you can still radiate positivity and wellness to others and receive the same. You are only preventing unnecessary and harmful negativity reaching you or adversely influencing you.

Whenever we are in a state of change, our energy fields become fragile. The reason for this is that with the old habitual patterns being released and new ones coming in, there is always a transition period where things are a little uncertain. These are the times when it is a good idea to make sure that our energy fields are as clear and strong as possible. Other than crystals, the Bach Flower Remedy, Walnut can be of help.

Clearing

Crystals can be used to help clear your aura from unwanted debris. Any irritations, minor unpleasantness or other negative occurrences in your daily life can remain lodged in your energy field. This includes thoughts and thought patterns of yourself and of others.

A quick and easy way to clear your energy field is to hold an appropriately tuned crystal (Snowy Quartz is excellent for this purpose) and imagine that you are standing under a waterfall of light. Visualise this light flowing through and around you, removing any impurities. Then see the light filling and replenishing you. You will, of course, need to ground yourself at the end. Anytime you take a physical shower, you could also focus on being cleansed on other levels. Those who prefer taking baths, could tune a small amount (a tablespoon or so) of Rock or Sea Salt for clearing and then add it to the bathwater. Most white crystals have a clearing energy as do Aquamarine, Blue Topaz, Apophyllite and Amethyst.

Another way to help clear negativity is to tune a crystal accordingly, and then either hold it, or (when sitting on a chair), place it on the floor in line with your spine. Afterwards, visualise any debris from your auric field flowing into the crystal. When finished, replenish yourself with light and ground yourself. Unpolished crystals which have an absorbing quality, such as Jasper or Black Tourmaline, can be very helpful for this. Please make sure you clean these crystals thoroughly afterwards.

Cleansing Breath

This is a highly effective technique for clearing, balancing and strengthening yourself. Stand straight, and breathe seven times around your energy field, each time moving further away (an inch or so) from your physical body. Start with the colour red (closest to the physical body) then orange, yellow, green, sky blue, indigo and end with a violet colour. Alternatively, you can just use 'white' light. On the in-breath, imagine the colour rising up from behind your feet, right up to over the top of your head. On the out-breath, imagine it flowing down the front of you into the earth, taking any debris with it. You could hold a Clear Quartz crystal to help you with this. As with all exercises, ground yourself at the end.

Energising

When you feel depleted, you can use crystals to help you regain energy. Tune two small Clear Quartz prisms or wands, and place one in the palm of each hand. One should have the tip pointing towards your wrist and the other towards your fingertips. It is best to place the crystal pointing towards you (tip towards the wrist) in your left hand and the other in your right hand. If, however, this feels uncomfortable and 'against the grain', change them around. By doing this exercise, you create a circuit of energy around you. Just sit for a little while and enjoy it. You can also tune a crystal with an uplifting quality to help you with your overall well-being, and then quietly sit with it for a while enjoying the energies. Please remember to ground yourself afterwards.

10

Self-Healing in a Pattern of Crystals

This is a technique where more than one crystal is needed. When placing crystals in a specific shape, you will not only be affected by the energy of the crystals but also by that of the shape. The aim, as always, is to opt for crystals that are harmonious and that can accentuate the chosen pattern. There is no need to use big crystals for this technique – tumblestones are fine.

The square: for this you will need four crystals. A square, just like a cube, has a grounding effect, and this technique would be excellent if you feel spaced out or ungrounded. Crystals with a denser energy are suitable for this. You could place the crystals at the four feet of a chair or in a square at your feet. When placing crystals around you in a bigger square, they need to have a higher energy. Lapis Lazuli, Sodalite and Fluorite are suitable for this since they have a cubic inner geometry and carry a high energy. They do, however, have a grounding quality on higher levels, such as helping to ground higher wisdom, ease mental stress and anchor inspiration respectively.

The triangle: this shape can help to energise you, provided appropriate crystals are selected. Clear Quartz, Citrine or equivalent energies would be suitable. Please do not forget to also use two grounding crystals, placed at your feet.

A **circle** and an **oval** shape around you would require six to eight crystals and could help protect your auric field or enhance it, depending on the crystals you use. Most crystals would be suitable for this (except those with a dense and grounding energy). It is advisable to use identical crystals for these shapes so that you receive one specific energy.

An **equal-armed cross** symbolizes the balancing of energies. If you wish to use this pattern, it is best to choose complementary crystals such as two Aventurine and two Rose Quartz or other crystals of a similar vibration. You can, however, use four identical crystals if you want to receive only one type of energy. As with all shapes (except the square), you will also need two grounding crystals.

Stars are also potent shapes, although for some, they may have religious connotations. Many find the five-pointed star highly protective, provided the top of the star is above your head when lying down, or in front of you when sitting on a chair. The six-pointed star is also considered a protective symbol as well as one that represents profound inner wisdom. High energy crystals are appropriate for stars.

The way to use this technique is to, first of all, cleanse and tune the crystals (for your highest good), then place them in the required pattern, and draw in the pattern with your hand. Next, sit within the pattern, and just as in the self-healing meditation, link to a light vibration, letting this energy fill you, the crystals, and the space you are sitting in. Afterwards, ground yourself thoroughly, dismantle the pattern and cleanse all the crystals. Please note that meditating with one crystal, fashioned into one of the above-mentioned shapes, will have a similar effect.

More Self-Healing using Patterns

By placing a few small crystals or tumblestones in an attractive arrangement on a table, you could create a specific 'note' of energy, representing a quality such as peace, harmony or joy. You could then tune this arrangement to enhance your environment and leave it until you feel the need to either change or dismantle it. An alternative, would be to group a few compatible crystals in a small circular pattern, and once happy with the overall note, tune them for your own wellbeing, take in the energy and then dismantle it. As with all crystal work, please do not forget to ground yourself afterwards.

If a loved one must leave you for a while, why not tune two identical tumblestones for harmony and support.

Give one to your beloved and keep the other near.

And whenever you are sad, it will bring you comfort.

11

Other Techniques

Chakra Healing Technique

I have not included chakra healing techniques with crystals (apart from an introduction to the solar plexus), because such work would require a certain amount of expertise. Chakras are spinning vortexes of energy situated in our bio-field. They relate to our life lessons and experiences, and according to what is going on in our lives, they can be blocked, spinning too slow or too fast, traumatised, or be in an acute state of change. Each of these states would require different crystalline energies to help create more balance, hence it is not possible to generalise on this. I have made an exception in regard to the solar plexus, which is a chakra situated roughly five centimetres above your navel. When you prod your stomach in that area, it will feel quite tender – the centre of the solar plexus is just above that spot. This is also the place where you can experience what is termed as a 'gut feeling'.

The solar plexus relates to, amongst other characteristics, our ego, self-esteem, fear, anger, personal power and control issues. Intense fear and anger, panic, or feeling over-wrought could indicate that this centre needs calming down. Feelings of low self-esteem, being unable to say no, or feeling weak and powerless when around those who are strong, could indicate that this centre is in need of a boost or strengthening.

You could briefly place a cleaned and tuned tumblestone on the solar plexus to help address such issues. For a boost, crystals such as Citrine, Clear Quartz and Sunstone have an uplifting, energising and strengthening quality, respectively. For calming, Yellow Jasper, Amber or Rose Quartz have an allaying, softening and calming energy in that order. These are just a few examples of the many crystals that relate to the solar plexus, so please only work with those you like and let your intuition guide you.

It is actually not necessary to place crystals directly on your chakras. If you need a lift in self-esteem, just hold the Citrine, Sunstone (or a crystal with similar qualities), relax and then focus on taking in the energies for a couple of minutes. You could imagine you are breathing the energy into your solar plexus area. Do not forget to ground afterwards and to cleanse the crystal you used.

Inner Development

The more we work with crystals and energy, the more we will find out about ourselves. Sometimes our life lessons are easy and joyful, yet at other times they may be more challenging. It is all a learning process. It can be useful to choose one specific crystal to help you as you move forward on your life path. Choose it with care, and whenever you feel the need, you can quietly sit with this crystal and reflect upon what is going on. Usually, crystals of a slightly higher vibration are appropriate for this. Just make sure you are grounded after you have finished with your inner work.

Affirmations using Crystals

An affirmation is a positive statement about something you may wish to do, become or change. It is best to restrict an affirmation to one or two sentences and then repeat these often. Tuning a crystal for this can help anchor the intent. Keep your affirmation in the present tense and make sure that the aim is realistic, achievable, and something for which you are willing to make the effort. For example, your affirmation could be, 'I am confident and at peace with myself'. This is fine, provided you are willing to look at what you may need to change in order to accomplish this! For this specific affirmation, you could tune a Ruby (representing confidence because it is vibrant and has a grounding quality) and Blue Lace Agate (because it has a gentle and peaceful energy).

Pendulum Aid

This is a technique that can help speed up the natural healing process in regard to small cuts, stings or similar 'emergency' issues. You will need a small and sturdy pendulum that you can swing rapidly around. It must be well-made, with the crystal firmly attached to a fairly short chain. If you cut yourself and have disinfected the area, you can take the pendulum and first of all establish a 'healthy' swing. The way to do this is to just ask, 'what is a healthy swing for me' and the pendulum will rotate either clockwise or anticlockwise.

You then hold the pendulum over the cut where it will turn in the opposite (unhealthy) direction. You then swing the pendulum quickly and deliberately in the healthy direction, directly over the cut. Check from time to time if the pendulum will swing by itself in the healthy direction, and when it does, you can stop the exercise. This technique is especially useful in the kitchen if you have been a little too clumsy with a knife. It can assist the natural healing process in kicking in that much faster. It can also help with bruises, scars and stings.

If you have an old scar, you could first establish your 'healthy direction' of the pendulum and then hold it over the scar. If it swings in the healthy direction, the technique will not be of any use, but if it swings in the 'unhealthy direction' you can do the exercise as outlined before. As with all such exercises, just imagine or ask for a natural healing energy to flow through you whilst you are doing it, and make sure you ground yourself when you have finished.

Energising your Water with Crystals

It is always a good idea to mentally clear and then tune your drinking water (as you do with a crystal) for your highest good. Rather than placing crystals in the water, you could instead tune them accordingly and put them around the container for a little while. Beryls, especially Aquamarine, are highly suitable for energising water since their inner geometry is hexagonal (as is Ice). The author does not recommend placing crystals in drinking water since many are slightly toxic and people sometimes swallow them by accident.

Jewellery

Once you know more about the specific energies of crystals, you can also use your jewellery to help you in your daily life. If you feel low in energy, you can wear one of the more uplifting crystals; if you feel vulnerable, you can use one that strengthens your energy. When stressed or spaced out, you can wear calming or grounding gemstones, and when you lack in confidence, wear something that gives you a personal boost. You only need to tune your piece of jewellery accordingly. Also, remember that metals can be used as crystals. Silver is protective in the way that it deflects energies, Gold is both strengthening and energising, and Copper is absorbent and grounding.

PART III

CRYSTAL SELECTION & QUALITIES

12

CRYSTAL LIST

The following list will show some of the many crystals that are used in healing. It has been categorised according to crystal families. When not in alphabetical order, specific crystals in the families have been listed according to the best known varieties.

Please note that this is only a very basic and general outline of the energies of each crystal. The reader is strongly urged to use his or her own intuition in choosing crystals, which will not only prove to be more effective, but also very enjoyable!

Quartz Family

Aventurine, Amethyst, Blue Lace Agate, Botswana Agate, Carnelian, Citrine, Clear Quartz, Jasper (including Mookite and Orbicular Jasper), Moss Agate, Rose Quartz, Smokey Quartz, Strawberry Quartz and Tigers Eye. The inner atomic structure of Quartz is trigonal.

Aventurine: Aventurine comes in green, blue and light orange colours. The green variety is the best-known and contains tiny specks of Mica, which gives it a sparkling appearance. Green Aventurine is best described as being complementary to Rose Quartz. Where Rose Quartz is yin, Aventurine is yang. Healers often use these two crystals together. Aventurine also has balancing and stabilising qualities.

Amethyst: In ancient times, Amethyst was thought to help prevent drunkenness, hence it was used to fashion goblets for drinking wine. Its colour is caused by inclusions of ferric oxide and ranges from a deep purple to a pale lilac. Considered to be a spiritual stone, it is widely used for meditation purposes and for help with insomnia, stress or nightmares. It is also one of the crystals that can help protect and clear the energy field from negativity. The colour can fade if placed for too long in strong sunlight. It is the complementary crystal to Citrine.

Blue Lace Agate: This Agate has a soft, gentle cooling and also clearing energy. Meditating with it can help induce a calm and relaxed state of being, especially if one also focuses on the colour vibration. It is an excellent crystal to help address and ease any stress-induced and overwrought conditions. One of the keywords for this crystal is peace.

Botswana Agate: Botswana Agate is a grey, brown and white layered crystal. It also comes in pink and grey, or pink and white, and the energies are quite slow and grounding. This crystal can symbolize the need for letting go of old and outworn patterns, and it aids this process, especially if used together with Snowy Quartz.

Carnelian: Carnelian has been used for thousands of years in jewellery. Its colour varies from deep red to orange or peach. A brown variety also exists and is called Sard. Traditionally, it was known to be a protective stone, and it can help ground one's energies as well as enhance creativity. It is complementary to many blue or turquoise crystals such as Chrysocolla, Lapis Lazuli (if the Carnelian is a deep red), Chalcedony and Blue Lace Agate.

Citrine: Natural Citrine is very rare. Most Citrine available on the market is heat-treated Amethyst or Smokey Quartz. It exists in pale yellow to a deep brown colour, has a very lively and sunny energy, and is often associated with joy and mental clarity. In healing, it can be used to uplift, energise and help regain a zest for life. A mixture of Citrine and Amethyst is known as Ametrine and carries the healing properties of both crystals.

Clear Quartz: Quartz is the most common crystal on the planet, and it exists in a multitude of colours. These various shades are caused by trace elements or other inclusions. It also has the unusual property of being piezoelectric (sensitive to pressure). Clear Quartz, which is transparent in colour, is considered to be a master healer because of its versatility. Not only is it highly energising, but it can also help in clearing blockages. It is also one of several crystals that can help with focus and concentration. Inclusions of Black Tourmaline, (Tourmalinated Quartz) or Rutile (Rutilated Quartz), within the Quartz, can alter the healing qualities of this master crystal. Tourmalinated Quartz is particularly effective in helping to minimise the negative emanations of electrical appliances. For clearing persistent blockages or purifying the auric field, many healers use the brilliant white variety of Quartz, called Milky or Snowy Quartz.

Jasper: Jasper comes in many different colours. The main ones used in healing are red, green and yellow. The green variety sometimes shows red specks and is called Bloodstone. Jasper has a fairly dense yet friendly energy; therefore, it is often used as an earthing or absorbing stone. Because it is grounding, it can help inspire confidence and strength. The yellow variety, in particular, can calm and sooth fearful and panicky conditions.

Mookaite: Mookaite is an Australian Jasper which also comes in a variety of colours such as magenta, yellow and purple, or a combination of these. The energy of Mookaite is a little softer than the other Jaspers.

Orbicular Jasper: This stone was discovered a few years ago, in a mine at the end of a beach, in Madagascar, which has now closed. The 'New Age' name is Ocean Jasper. Since then, another mine has been discovered, where Polychrome Jasper can be found. Both types of Jasper consist of a multitude of colours, and each specimen is slightly different. Their energies are lighter than ordinary Jasper and have a calming and slightly uplifting effect. The energies of these Jaspers can be helpful in regard to matters of confidence, stress and balance.

Moss Agate: This crystal is deep green combined with white and/or light blue areas. It is often slightly translucent. Its energy can be described as fairly solid and balancing, and meditating with it can remind one of being in nature. It is also one of the crystals that can help address emotional stress, and in this context, it works well together with Blue Lace Agate.

Rose Quartz: The colour of Rose Quartz is caused by traces of manganese or titanium. It has a very gentle although profound energy and may be of help with all matters relating to love, nurturing and harmony. It can also help support those who have suffered from any kind of abuse or who have a condition that requires a safe and kind energy. It is suitable for the fragile, the very young or old, and for animals.

Smokey Quartz: Smokey Quartz is a very powerful crystal. It comes in light and dark grey, brown, and black. Sometimes, a specimen for sale is actually artificially irradiated Rock Crystal; if this is the case, it may be unpleasant to touch. If natural, however, it can be of help in clearing any form of negativity as well as assessing and addressing deep inner fears. It also has a grounding energy and works well together with Snowy Quartz. It is not to be used lightly.

Strawberry Quartz: This light pink crystal has grey or black inclusions and is slightly translucent. The energies are slightly denser than Rose Quartz and could indicate a need for self-nurturing or self-care. It can look similar to pale pink Rhodonite but is much lighter in energy. It is complementary to Moss Agate.

Tigers Eye: Yellow or golden Tigers Eye and Hawks Eye (the deep blue variety), are mainly found in South Africa. Both are thought to carry a protective energy on mundane (yellow) or more subtle (blue) levels. The golden variety has a warming as well as earthy energy, whereas the midnight blue version can be of help in easing tensions and aches. A red variety is often heat-treated yellow Tigers Eye. Another crystal called Tiger Iron is a combination of Jasper, Hematite and Tigers Eye. This crystal is a heavy-duty grounder.

~♦~

Feldspar Family

Amazonite, Labradorite, Moonstone, Sunstone, Unakite. The inner atomic structure of feldspar ranges from monoclinic to triclinic.

Amazonite: Although also of the Feldspar Family, this crystal has very different properties from the others. Its colour is green, sometimes slightly turquoise, and its energy is fairly solid. It can be of help when feeling a little run down and in need of strength. The darker variety is from Russia and the lighter coloured stones are from Brazil. It does not really combine that well with many other crystals except Rhodonite. The reason for this could be that both crystals have the same inner geometry. Amazonite is triclinic.

Labradorite: This stunning crystal grows in layers. The blue, blue/green and sometimes orange and yellow 'shiller' effect is caused by the reflection of light on the various layers. It has a profound energy, which can help one reach a deep level of stillness and meditation. A brighter variety, called Spectrolite, is found in Finland. Moonstone, Sunstone and Labradorite all have a magical quality and work extremely well together. This crystal is triclinic.

Moonstone: Moonstone has a beautiful silvery sheen, and the variety with a bluish lustre has often been favoured in jewellery. Traditionally, it is associated with its name as well as the feminine, the mysterious and the psychic. It has a soft and flowing energy and can be of help with emotional issues, stress, and personal as well as psychic development. It can also help to find the path of least resistance. Meditating with the black variety, however, can bring deep seated fears or other challenging personal issues to the fore. Moonstone is monoclinic.

Sunstone: The colour of this crystal is a deep burnt orange with a golden sheen. It has tiny inclusions of Hematite which cause the 'shiller' effect. Sunstone has a warm and powerful energy, which beautifully balances the more flowing and feminine energy of Moonstone. Healers often use these crystals together because they complement so well. Sunstone is triclinic.

Unakite: Unakite is a combination of green Epidote and pink Feldspar. Green and pink are complementary colours, and this crystal does have a balancing effect. The energies, however, are rather slow, and like Amazonite, it does not really work well with many other crystals except Clear Quartz, Rose Quartz and Moonstone. It can also be used for gentle grounding. Unakite is monoclinic.

~♦~

Beryl Family

Aquamarine, Emerald, Golden Beryl, Goshenite and Bixbite, and Morganite. The inner atomic structure of Beryls is hexagonal.

Aquamarine: Aquamarine belongs to the Beryl family. The name means 'water from the sea' (Latin), probably so named because of its blue/green colour. It has a very fine and clearing energy which is uplifting without being invasive. The inner geometry of all Beryls is identical to ice, which is why the energy of these crystals can be very suitable for energising and enhancing water. Meditating with Aquamarine can help clear, boost and refresh your energy field.

Emerald: This is a more expensive cousin of Aquamarine and is considered to be one of the few precious gemstones. It has a brilliant green colour, and the best quality Emerald comes from Columbia. Healers will use a lesser quality Emerald, not only because it is more affordable, but because polished, high-grade precious gemstones (as used in jewellery) can be too intense for use in certain parts of the subtle energy field. The energies of Emerald are highly potent.

Golden Beryl: This crystal looks similar to Citrine, and like other Beryls, has a more profound yet subtle energy than Quartz. Maybe the reason for this is that the inner geometry of Beryls is hexagonal, whereas Quartz is trigonal. The hexagonal form is more balanced since the top and bottom are the same. Golden Beryl is uplifting and has a sunny energy, but reaches deeper levels than Citrine. A greenish yellow variety is called Heliodore.

Goshenite and Bixbite are clear and red Beryls respectively. These crystals are not all that common, which is why they are not written about separately. An interesting characteristic of Bixbite is that the element of water is not involved in its formation. Clearing and grounding are some of the qualities of these crystals.

Morganite: This pink crystal looks very similar to Rose Quartz. It has, however, a more profound as well as potent energy and is complementary to Emerald. Both crystals (and Golden Beryl) can be of help in addressing and balancing issues relating to qualities of the heart, but they work on a far deeper and more subtle level than Rose Quartz, Aventurine or Citrine.

~♦~

Tourmaline Family

Schorl, Indicolite, Verdelite, Water Melon, Rubellite, Dravite and Elbaite. The inner atomic structure of tourmaline is trigonal.

Tourmaline comes in a wide variety of colours. It is pyroelectric (sensitive to heat) as well as piezoelectric, and it does have a very intense and indeed 'electric' energy. It is a powerful healing crystal which works to the point of greatest need on all levels: from the spiritual right down to the etheric. It can also help address old scars on physical, emotional and mental levels.

Schorl, the black variety, is excellent for heavy duty grounding and for absorbing any form of negativity. Most healers use it to counteract geopathic stress from computers or other electrical devices. For personal protection, which is about creating a strong auric field, crystals of much higher vibrations are indicated.

Indicolite is blue, **Verdelite** is green, **Water Melon** is a combination of green and pink, **Rubellite** is a deep pink, **Dravite** is brown and **Elbaite** is clear. All these crystals have a powerful and intense energy. There are many more different coloured Tourmalines that are used in jewellery and for healing. Please note, that because of its potency, this crystal is not particularly suitable for the fragile.

~♦~

Calcites

Calcite: Calcite is a soft mineral which exists in a variety of colours. It has a soothing as well as absorbing quality and is very versatile. It is widely used in healing and can help with all kinds of upheavals and change. The red, orange and honey-coloured Calcites are warming, stabilising and uplifting. The blue and green ones are more cooling, balancing and inspiring. Those that are white can help to release and clear, and those that are pink have a nurturing energy that is softer than Rose Quartz. The energies, although fairly solid, are so gentle that it is an excellent crystal to use for those who are fragile and for whom a more potent energy would be too much.

Optical Calcite: These translucent Calcites are completely different from their opaque cousins and have a much faster and intense energy. They come in various colours such as yellow, pale pink, pale green and clear. A brownish yellow, or sometimes clear variety, which forms in beautiful geometrical shapes, is called Dogtooth Calcite (the new age name is Stellar Beam Calcite). Occasionally, it can be found growing together with Hematite. All Calcites are trigonal.

~♦~

Corundum

Ruby and Sapphire

Ruby: Ruby is also considered to be one of the precious gemstones. Its colour ranges from a deep brilliant red to a light pink. With its vibrant and solid energy, it can promote confidence, vitality and stability. It is often used as the centre stone of engagement rings. In healing, a less potent quality is usually applied. Both Ruby and Sapphire are trigonal.

Sapphire: Sapphire is another of the precious gemstones. It comes in a variety of colours although the deep blue version is the most widely known. Like Emerald, Ruby and Diamond, it is often fashioned into stunning jewellery. Sapphires used for healing are usually of a lighter blue colour than the gem quality. The energies of this crystal are potent and can help with creativity, communication issues, and accessing inner wisdom.

~♦~

Garnet Family

The Garnet family is extremely complicated, and these crystals come in many different types and a multitude of colours. For the purpose of this book, only a few of these are mentioned. All Garnets are cubic.

Red Garnet: This is the most commonly known type of Garnet. The deep red ones that are fashioned into jewellery are usually Pyrope Garnets. The same deep red, but a lesser quality, called Almandine, is usually used for healing. The energies are very profound and deeply transformative, but also grounding. Hence, this crystal is not used on the finer levels of the auric field. Spessartine Garnet has a more yellowish orange lustre.

Green Garnet: There are many different varieties of green Garnet. They are complementary to red Garnets and have a similar energy. Both Red and Green Garnet can be used to anchor energies and to help manifest necessary changes. The green Garnets are also very stabilizing.

Black Garnet: This crystal, named Melanite, is usually only suitable for grounding. Its energy is very heavy and not really applied in the auric field other than beneath the feet. Meditating with Melanite can bring one's deepest fears to light, which is not for the faint-hearted, especially since one then has to deal with the outcome.

~♦~

Gypsum Family

Alabaster, Desert Rose, Satin Spar and Selenite. All of these crystals are monoclinic.

Alabaster: Alabaster comes in a variety of greens and browns, and forms in masses. Orange Alabaster looks similar to Carnelian but has a more subtle quality to it. It works harmoniously in combination with the other crystals of the Gypsum family.

Desert Rose: This is a light brown, (sometimes tinged with white), crystal, which forms in florets and consists of crystallized sand. It has a gentle, warm and light vibration, and healers often use it as an anchor for the higher energies of Selenite and Satin Spar.

Satin Spar: This has almost identical qualities to Selenite. The crystals form in shining white fibrous masses and are opaque. Purity is a good term to describe the quality of Satin Spar. It works on more subtle levels than Snowy Quartz and Blue Topaz.

Selenite: This is a clear to white, partly transparent crystal. It can form in a jagged shape called 'Fishtail' or as elongated, flat crystals. The energies are very fine and can help to link to Universal energies such as the Angelic. It also has a clearing quality and can be used for this purpose on the higher levels within the auric field.

~♦~

Spodumene

Kunzite and Hiddenite. The inner atomic structure of these crystals is monoclinic.

Kunzite: Kunzite is a pale lilac/pink, translucent crystal. It has a very fine, high and subtle energy. **Hiddenite**, the clear variety, has a tinge of green caused by traces of chromium. Both these crystals complement each other beautifully and are used by healers on the higher mental and spiritual levels in the auric field.

~♦~

Topaz

Topaz is mainly found in a golden, golden pink, blue or clear colour. The pink variety is named Imperial Topaz. The blue variety is often unnaturally irradiated. Golden Topaz has a wonderful, strong and warming energy which is uplifting and inspiring. In contrast, the blue variety has an extremely fast as well as clearing energy, with a 'hard' quality similar to ice. Both the clear and the blue variety can help release negativity and blockages on emotional, mental and spiritual levels in quite a forceful manner! Topaz is orthorhombic.

~ ♦ ~

Other Healing Crystals

The following crystals are one of a kind and therefore not grouped into families. These have been placed in alphabetical order.

Amber: Amber is an organic mineral, mainly found in areas around the Baltic Sea. It is a fossilised tree resin that can be over three hundred million years old, and like Obsidian, it is amorphous. Highly regarded since ancient times, it was once worth its weight in gold. Blessed with a warm, friendly and gentle energy, it can be used for any condition that needs soothing and easing. It is also suitable for the very frail, young or old, as well as for extreme conditions.

Apophyllite: This is a clear/white crystal that is semi-transparent. It forms in clusters and often has inclusions of Stilbite (a pink crystal). It has a high water content. The energies of Apophyllite are quite fast and flowing, and the crystals can be of help in clearing blockages and negativity in the auric field as well as in the environment. Apophyllite is tetragonal.

Aragonite: This crystal is light brown with a hint of Nacre, which makes it a distant cousin of pearl. It looks a little like a 'sputnik' with many interlinking tiny tubes. It has quite a light-hearted energy and works well with Abalone, Coral, Blue Topaz and some of the higher frequency crystals. Aragonite is Orthorhombic.

Azurite: This is a striking, deep and brilliant blue crystal, often found growing together with Malachite. Its energy is fairly fast and potent. Meditating with it can help promote inner vision. Because of its colour, it can also help protect the auric field against lower and negative vibrations. Azurite is monoclinic.

Celestite: Celestite is another soft crystal, pale blue or white in colour. The blue variety is found in Madagascar. Its gentle colour is deceptive, since the energy of Celestite is fast and powerful. This crystal can help connect with, and reach, angelic and spiritual realms. In healing, it is frequently used as a cleanser of negativity and worn-out patterns, helping to integrate the new. When meditating with Celestite, it is essential to use a grounding crystal in order to avoid being 'spaced out'. Aragonite is one of the crystals that complements it beautifully. Celestite is orthorhombic.

Chrysocolla: This crystal is sometimes difficult to distinguish from Turquoise. It has a lovely deep green/blue colour and often grows together with Malachite. Its strong energy can help address issues with communication or 'feeling under the weather'. Many feel that it can also help with all kinds of creativity. Its inner structure is monoclinic.

Copper: This crystal is very helpful as a conductor of energy. Many people wear a copper bracelet in order to help with rheumatism. In healing, it is usually used to help ground, draw out or distribute energies. Copper is cubic.

Danburite: This is a very pale pink, translucent crystal with a fine, high and fast energy. Danburite can help create a link to the angelic and to one's own soul qualities. As with all high energy crystals, it is recommended you use a grounding stone whilst meditating with it. Red Garnet, Green Garnet and Peridot are all equally suitable for this. Danburite is orthorhombic.

Diamond: Diamonds have evolved from Carbon, a substance derived from the plant kingdom. Maybe this is the reason that their energies are so different from other crystals and gemstones. They are the hardest (10 on the Mohs Scale) of all the crystals and are not often used in healing, because apart from being very expensive, their energies are extremely concentrated and intense. In one sense, Diamonds can symbolize greed and materialism; on the other hand, they also stand for eternal love and romance. Like a mirror, they can relate to our own shadows as well as our good qualities, and this can help us develop. Maybe once we have cleared and polished all of our own facets, we will sparkle as brilliantly as a Diamond! Small Diamonds surrounding a larger gemstone intensify the energies of the latter. If you have Diamond jewellery and tune it for your highest good, it can enhance your own energy and well-being. Diamonds are cubic.

Dumortierite: This is a dark blue crystal containing black specks. Though difficult to distinguish from Sodalite, its energy is lighter and does not have grounding qualities, which is why it can be applied on all levels in the auric field. It has a protective element, and meditating with it can help ease mental stress. It can also be used to help release persistent nightmares. Its inner geometry is orthorhombic.

Fluorite: Fluorite comes in many colours. The most frequently used, in the field of healing, are purple, green, blue, clear and yellow. Fluorite is inspiring, has a magical quality and hence is excellent for use in meditation. It can help bring insights gained in deep meditation to consciousness since it has a very subtle grounding quality on the more spiritual levels. In addition, it is effective in easing disturbed sleep or dream patterns. Its beauty is healing and uplifting in itself. Its structure is cubic. The (combined) blue and yellow variety is called Blue John.

Gold: Gold is not all that often used in healing, mainly because it is so expensive. It has an uplifting and potent energy. It can also absorb energies, and, therefore, it is important to clear it frequently. Should you be given jewellery that has belonged to someone else, please take some time to do an in-depth cleansing of the piece in question, and then tune it for your highest good. It is advisable to clear jewellery that you wear on a daily basis. Gold is cubic.

Halite: Halite is also known as Rock Salt. The reason it is used in healing is that, like all forms of natural Salt, it has a clearing quality. If placed in water it would dissolve, so please use another method to clean it! Halite is cubic and comes in many different colours.

Hematite: This is a fairly dense and heavy-duty grounding crystal. The colour is Silver with an inner core of red (iron oxide). It is extremely solid. Hematite is trigonal. Hematoid Quartz is Clear Quartz with a reddish tint caused by inclusions of hematite. It is quite energising.

Herkimer Diamond: Herkimer Diamonds belong to the Quartz family. They are slightly harder than Quartz and only found in County Herkimer in the States. Most of them are small, and all are double terminated. Their energies are a little brighter and more intense than Clear Quartz.

Jade: Jade exists in many colours. The best known are green, lilac, white and black. Many ornaments, such as small bowls or containers, figurines or statues of animals, are fashioned from Jade. In healing, the dark to mid-green variety is generally used as this has a smooth and balancing energy. The black variety is excellent for meditation and will help you to find that point of inner stillness and just 'be'. Jade is monoclinic.

Jet: Jet is technically not a crystal: it is basically ancient rotted tree matter. In the Victorian age, it was often worn as jewellery in times of grief and bereavement. Its energies are kind and also gently grounding. Jet is amorphous.

Kyanite: Kyanite is also called Disthene, which means 'double strength'. This is because the hardness of Kyanite is different across its width as it is along its length. It mainly comes in blue, green and grey. The energies of Kyanite are powerful, and of the three colours mentioned, the grey variety is the most potent, followed by the blue and then the green. This crystal is triclinic and is indicative of huge inner transformation.

Lapis Lazuli: Lapis Lazuli (meaning blue stone) is a rock consisting of several minerals. Popular since ancient times, it was fashioned into ornaments as well as jewellery in Egypt. It was also ground to create blue pigment in paints. It can be of help with protection, meditation and regression (looking into your past) as well as accessing ancient knowledge. Focusing on the deep blue colour has also been known to promote calm and ease pain. The golden specks in good quality Lapis are Pyrite. Lapis is cubic.

Lepidolite: Lepidolite is a beautiful stone that comes in a variety of colours. The specimens used for healing are pale to dark violet/purple with inclusions of Mica. The energy of this stone can be likened to a softer version of Amethyst, with the Mica giving it a magical quality. Like all purple stones, it has a protective quality and would be excellent for dreamwork. The inner structure is monoclinic.

Malachite: This is a well-known crystal that has always been used to create beautiful objects and jewellery. It has a high copper content, and although it carries a potent energy, it is physically soft. It has been used for healing in many cultures and was traditionally thought to help with eye problems and conditions of the womb. Malachite can also be of help in bringing stubborn negative emotions to the fore in order to be cleared. Its energy is intense and fairly dense; so it must be used with great care. The inner structure is monoclinic.

Obsidian: Obsidian is a volcanic glass and amorphous. It is one of the oldest known and used stones, and in the past, was fashioned into knives, spears and arrowheads. The black variety was also made into spheres for scrying. It is said that Nostradamus used an Obsidian mirror to glimpse the future. In healing, Obsidian can help to bring deeply hidden issues to light; it is also sometimes used to ground energies. Not only is it suitable for deep meditation, but it can also ease tensions and pain. The brown variety is called Mahogany Obsidian and is mainly used for grounding. Snowflake Obsidian, which is black with white specks, has a lighter energy and often symbolizes the light at the end of the tunnel!

Pearl: Although Pearl is technically not a crystal, it is often used in healing and has a beautiful, soft and luminous energy. It is particularly useful for those who are fragile, and it can be combined with shell in order to ease and gently repair issues. It also combines well with Opal, or Aquamarine if a slightly more potent energy is appropriate. Pearl and Aragonite also work well together since both have Nacre as a component.

Peridot: Peridot (pronounced without the t) is a deep to light green crystal. The lesser quality is called Olivine. Like Garnet and Jet, it was often worn as jewellery in Victorian times. Its energies are quite profound, although lighter than green Garnet. In meditation, this crystal can help link to the energies of nature, folklore and the Devic kingdom. It is also balancing and works extremely well with Blue Topaz which has the same inner geometric structure (orthorhombic).

Prehnite: This is a light green crystal, sometimes containing tiny flecks of brown or black. It is similar to Aventurine, although a little smoother and lighter in energy. When used to address emotional stress, it works beautifully together with Rose Quartz. It is orthorhombic.

Pyrite: Also known as Fool's Gold, it emits sparks when struck, and the name originates from the Greek word for fire. It forms as cubic crystals, and in healing, it can be used for grounding as well as energising. It can also help with manifesting ideas and developing more focus, confidence and optimistm. Pyrite is cubic.

Realgar: This is a beautiful, vibrant orange/red crystal that consists mainly of arsenic, so it is highly poisonous. It is rarely used by healers but is worth mentioning because it is so beautiful! It is monoclinic.

Rhodochrosite: This crystal ranges from a brilliant red to a light pink colour. It has a strong and potent energy. The pale pink coloured crystals can address issues relating to heart qualities, whereas the red variety is more suitable for helping with matters of vitality, self-belief and power. Its inner structure is trigonal.

Rhodonite: Rhodonite is a pink and black crystal with a fairly gentle yet heavy energy. It is usually used for grounding. Some would say that it can also help to ground (and thereby manifest) qualities of the heart. In healing, it is not used on the finer levels of the auric field. Rhodonite is triclinic.

Silver: Although not often used in healing, it is worthwhile mentioning, since there is much jewellery fashioned from this metal. Silver can help deflect unhelpful energies, and it also relates to the mysterious, the feminine and the moon. Like most metals, it is cubic.

Sodalite: This crystal, dark blue in colour, is one of the components of Lapis Lazuli. Sometimes it contains white inclusions of Calcite. Its protective and stabilising qualities originate from its solid and powerful energy. Sodalite can also help to draw out qualities of focus, confidence, determination and strength, that are needed to manifest ideas and plans. It is fantastic for mental stress, clearing blockages and easing pain. Sodalite is cubic.

Sugilite: This crystal was discovered in the nineteen seventies, in South Africa, at the same time as the planet Chiron. The highest grade is a deep purple. It has a powerful and profound energy and is not to be used lightly. It harmonizes with golden or yellow crystals such as Golden Beryl and Topaz, or can be softened by combining it with Amber. It also has a protective energy, and like most purple crystals, it is helpful with meditation. Its inner structure is hexagonal.

Sulphur: This is a bright yellow crystal that is fairly fragile. It is easily recognisable since it smells strongly of matches. It is mainly used to help clear stubborn energies from certain parts within the auric field, and its inner structure is orthorhombic.

Turquoise: This ancient stone was first known to be mined in Persia (now called Iran), thousands of years ago. It was mainly sold in Turkey, from which the name derives, and has been used in many cultures for healing. Traditionally, it was known as a protective stone and was often fashioned into amulets. It can be of help with communication and to clear out, as well as ward off, any form of negativity. It can also help to strengthen the whole system. On a deeper level, it is sometimes used to link to ancestral energies. It combines beautifully with Sunstone. Turquoise is triclinic.

13

Visual Guide to Crystals

The next few pages provide a visual guide to identifying most of the common crystals you will have read about earlier in this book.

Quartz and Feldspar Crystals

Aventurine

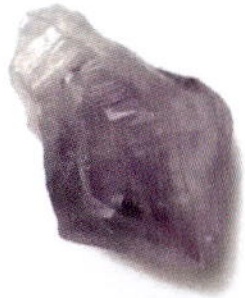
Amethyst

Blue Lace Agate

Botswana Agate

Carnelian

Citrine

Clear Quartz

Red, Yellow, Green Jasper

Mookite

Orbicular Jasper

Moss Agate

Rose Quartz

Smokey Quartz

Strawberry Quartz

Blue & Gold Tigers Eye

Amazonite

Labradorite

Moonstone

Sunstone

Unakite

Beryl, Tourmaline, Calcite and Corundum Crystals

Aquamarine

Emerald

Golden Beryl

Morganite

Schorl (Black Tourmaline)

Dravite and Indicolite Tourmalines

Water Melon Tourmaline

Rubellite and Verdelite Tourmalines

Elbaite Tourmaline

Blue Calcite

Green Calcite

Honey Calcite

Orange Calcite

White/Clear Calcite

Septarian

Optical Calcite

Ruby

Sapphire

Garnet, Gypsum and Topaz Crystals

Red Garnet

Orange Garnet

Green Garnet

Black Garnet

Desert Rose

Satin Spar

Selenite

Kunzite

Hiddenite

Blue Topaz

Golden Topaz

Other Healing Crystals

Amber

Apophyllite

Aragonite

Azurite

Celestite

Chrysocolla

Copper

Danburite

Other Healing Crystals continued

Dumortierite

Fluorite

Hematite

Herkimer Diamond

Jade

Jet

Kyanite

Lapis Lazuli

Lepidolite

Malachite

Obsidian

Pearl

Peridot

Prehnite

Pyrite

Realgar

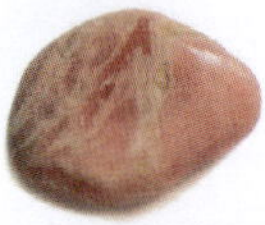
Rhodochrosite

Rhodonite

Sodalite

Sugilite

Sulphur

Turquoise

14

Easy Reference Lists

Grounding Crystals

This list of grounding crystals has been provided for easy reference. In order to establish which crystal can help you ground, pick one up and notice how it feels. If it is unpleasant, you should opt for a gentler one.

Potent grounding

- Black Tourmaline
- Chiastolite
- Galena
- Red and Green Garnet
- Black Garnet
- Hematite
- Obsidian
- Ruby
- Tiger Iron

Medium grounding

- Botswana Agate
- Carnelian
- Copper
- Jaspers
- Smokey Quartz
- Petrified Wood
- Pyrite
- Rhodonite
- Tigers Eye

Gentle grounding

- Amber
- Aragonite (dark)
- Desert Rose
- Jade (black & dark green)
- Jet
- Red and Orange Calcite
- Septarian
- Sunstone
- Unakite

Cleansing Crystals

All white crystals have a clearing energy. But do be aware that there are crystals of other colours, such as Amethyst, that also have this quality in addition to their other properties. Both types are listed below.

White Crystals

- Apophyllite
- Howlite
- Goshenite
- Moonstone
- Opal
- Satin Spar
- Scolecite
- Selenite
- Snowy Quartz
- White Calcite

Other Clearing Crystals

- Amethyst
- Aquamarine
- Blue Lace Agate
- Blue Topaz
- Botswana Agate
- Clear Quartz
- Lepidolite
- Smokey Quartz

- Malachite (draws out debris)
- Sulphur (draws out debris)

Protective Crystals

Crystals can also help strengthen our energy fields and are hence considered protective. Some of the 'traditional' ones are Turquoise, Lapis Lazuli, Sodalite, Amethyst and Hawks Eye. Most purple and violet crystals also have a protective quality, and Silver can help deflect negative energies.

A Final Consideration

The purpose of this book is to open a door for those who are drawn to crystals and who would like to know a little more about how to use them, safely and responsibly, in everyday life. Their beauty and undeniably beneficial energies can be enjoyed by all, and their gift to Humanity is immeasurable.

Working with crystals is not only an enriching experience but can often be life transforming. Please always treat your crystals with love, care and respect. Above all, do not practice on others without having a fully recognised qualification. It is also essential that you ensure your crystals are clean so that their energies remain dynamic.

For those who are interested in healing, it is important to know that being a healer is a way of life, a continuous journey, that is full of joy as well as challenges. No special talents are required to step upon this path. Healing is a gift that anyone who has a profound interest, as well as a sense of commitment and dedication, can develop. It does, however, take several years of training before one is ready to start practicing professionally, and the learning never stops!

Crystals can also be of help with the inevitable process of growth, facing and dealing with inner shadows, finding our truth, letting go of worn-out patterns, and above all, they open doors and create opportunities to enable us to fulfil our purpose. Many find it useful to keep a journal in order to jot down special experiences with their crystals.

May your journey with crystals be in light and joy!

Appendix I

MOHS' HARDNESS SCALE

All **Quartz** Crystals mentioned have a hardness of 7. Some of the **Agate**s may be slightly less. All the **Beryls** have a hardness of 8. The **Feldspars** are 6 - 6.5.

Amber 2.5
Alabaster 2
Aragonite 3.5 - 4
Apophyllite 4
Azurite 3.5 - 4
Calcite 3
Celestite 3 - 3.5
Chiastolite 7.5
Chrysocolla 3.5 - 4
Copper 2.5
Danburite 7
Desert Rose 2
Diamond 10
Fluorite 4
Galena 2.5
Garnet 6.5 - 7.5
Halite 2
Hematite 5-6
Herkimer Diamond 7.5
Hiddenite 6.5 - 7.5
Jade 6 - 7
Jet 2
Kunzite 6.5 - 7.5
Kyanite 4 -5 & 6 - 7
Lapis Lazuli 5.5 - 6
Lepidolite 2.5 - 4
Malachite 3.5 - 4
Moonstone 6 - 6.5
Obsidian 5
Peridot 6
Prehnite 6 - 6.5
Pyrite 6
Realgar 1.5
Rhodochrosite 3.5 - 4
Rhodonite 5.5 - 6.5
Ruby 9
Sapphire 9
Satin Spar 2
Selenite 2
Septarian 3
Silver 2.5
Sugilite 6
Topaz 8
Tourmaline 7.5
Turquoise 5

Appendix II

USEFUL INFORMATION

How can Crystal & Energy Healing be of Help?

Healing is mainly about addressing the cause of any imbalance that clients may be experiencing in their lives, thereby helping them move through relevant issues with a little more ease. The way this is done is by assessing the state of a client's auric field and the systems within it, and channeling natural energies where appropriate. Crystals and other tools may also be used in order to shape and focus the healing energies. So, if anything is out of kilter in your life, it could be worthwhile to have a healing session, where you may gain some relief, release old patterns, or obtain necessary insights or inspiration on what action to take. Please note that healing is complementary rather than an alternative to conventional medicine.

How do I find a Crystal Healer (Therapist) or Energy Healing Practitioner?

The Federation of Subtle Energy Medicine (FSEM) holds a list of accredited UK based practitioners on its web site. All practitioners on this register have been trained to the highest standards and completed a minimum of two years of training. Because of their expertise, they also hold a certificate in subtle energy medicine. Specialists in this field have completed a further two to three years of postgraduate studies. FSEM Healer members carry a therapist public liability and malpractice insurance, and adhere to the FSEM code of conduct.

Questions to ask a Complementary Therapist

Before you book a session with any complementary therapist, it is important that you are confident of their expertise. There are several questions you can ask the therapist you have chosen. You can enquire where they have trained, how long they have trained for, how long they have practiced, and if they belong to a regulatory or umbrella organisation. It is also a good idea to find out whether they are insured and what fees they charge. Then ask them to explain the therapy to you in lay terms if necessary. Any therapist worth their salt will be happy to answer such questions, to reassure you that you are in good hands.

ABOUT THE AUTHOR

Henriette Maasdijk is a Subtle Energy Medicine Specialist™ and De-stress therapist, and has completed the certificate of education (Cert.Ed). She is a founder of the Vibrational Healing Foundation and co-founder of the Federation of Subtle Energy Medicine. She is also a member of, and consultant to, several healing organisations. She has taught throughout the UK, Ireland and Europe for over 25 years, leading diploma courses and workshops on Subtle Energy Medicine subjects and inner development. She has always had a keen interest in the so-called unknown, and a great love and respect for the beauty and power of crystals. She believes that inner development and healing are the key to a life of joy, empowerment and fulfilment. Henriette is of Dutch origin and has lived in London for over thirty-five years.

About the Vibrational Healing Foundation

The VHF, formed in 1996, offers expert training in healing and inner development. In the ancient wisdom schools, the dictum 'man know thyself' conveyed best what such training represents; nowadays, it comes under the term 'subtle energy medicine'.

Subtle energy medicine, in a nutshell, is about the exploration of ourselves as complex beings of energy, existing in a world of energy, and how this relates to our life, health and wellbeing. It is also about being able to support others, when they need it, with the skilled use of tools such as crystals, flowers, flower remedies, colour and sound. Such work and study are an ongoing process, because this is also a path towards what is termed enlightenment.

For information on courses in the UK, please visit:

vibrationalhealingfoundation.co.uk

~~~

About the Federation of Subtle Energy Medicine

The Federation of Subtle Energy Medicine (FSEM) is an umbrella organization whose purpose is to set, and uphold, constant high professional standards of training and practice in healing and inner development. Members work in close co-operation, harmony and goodwill, maintaining individual styles and expertise, whilst adhering to FSEM Standards. All practitioners on the register are highly experienced and adhere to a strict code of conduct.

For information about regulations and to find a subtle energy medicine therapist or training school in the UK, please visit:

subtlehealth.org
~~~

Healing is a way of life.
Walk the path, to find
your truth.

And help others along
the way.

Printed in Great Britain
by Amazon

44109698R00069